# The Psyche Trials

*poems by*

# STEPHANIE LATERZA

*Finishing Line Press*
Georgetown, Kentucky

# The Psyche Trials

Copyright © 2019 by STEPHANIE LATERZA
ISBN 978-1-63534-954-2 First Edition
All rights reserved under International and Pan-American Copyright Conventions.
No part of this book may be reproduced in any manner whatsoever without written permission from the publisher, except in the case of brief quotations embodied in critical articles and reviews.

## ACKNOWLEDGMENTS

"Cherimoya Heart" (*L'Éphémère Review, Dalliance* Issue, April 2018)
"Homecoming" (*San Francisco Peace and Hope,* online 2016; printed anthology, *San Francisco Peace and Hope, Light The Sky*: 2018)
"Eros" (*Ovunque Siamo,* January 2018)
"Morning" (*Newtown Literary,* Winter 2015)
"Fire Leaves" (*San Francisco Peace and Hope,* online Issue 4-2014; printed anthology: 2015)
"Appendix Heart" (Stephanie Laterza—Author Wordpress blog, 2015)

Publisher: Leah Maines

Editor: Christen Kincaid

Cover Art: Stephanie Laterza

Author Photo: Stephanie Laterza

Cover Design: Elizabeth Maines McCleavy

Printed in the USA on acid-free paper.
Order online: www.finishinglinepress.com
also available on amazon.com

Author inquiries and mail orders:
Finishing Line Press
P. O. Box 1626
Georgetown, Kentucky 40324
U. S. A.

# Table of Contents

Eros ........................................................................................... 1
Morning ..................................................................................... 2
Vertical Connection ................................................................... 3
Guitar Strings ............................................................................ 4
Moon Crown .............................................................................. 5
For Eros, Love Psyche ............................................................... 6
The Bitter End ........................................................................... 7
Walking Around Cambridge ..................................................... 8
Sonnet in Contemplation of Hieronymus Bosch's *Death
and the Miser* ........................................................................ 9
In the Room ............................................................................. 10
The Same Cold ........................................................................ 11
Tapas ........................................................................................ 13
Homecoming ........................................................................... 14
Fire Leaves ............................................................................... 15
Simple Morning ....................................................................... 16
In the quiet .............................................................................. 17
Rain Arrangement .................................................................. 18
Doors ....................................................................................... 20
Anniversary ............................................................................. 22
Static ........................................................................................ 23
Star Drop ................................................................................. 24
The Day Before Valentine's Day ............................................. 25
Psyche's Sunday ...................................................................... 26
Vibrations ................................................................................ 27
Reservoirs ................................................................................ 28
Appendix Heart ....................................................................... 30
Cherimoya Heart ..................................................................... 31

*For my love*

**Eros**


The way pigeons fly in an upward vee
in the free pale dawn, I unbutton even my skin,
to become more naked,

sweat-glazed like the head
on a lily's pistil,

I breathe inside the hollow of your insides;
you breathe back—

I fold myself like a flattened rose
between your palms

because now
words don't need to come as often
because you have
found me as I have become, without history
it seems you have always been
feeding me water from your mouth,

I have learned the ocean
is a familiar blue
mirror held up to the sky,
holding the whole horizon.

## Morning

I mistook your arm for my thigh,
in the morning,
the way we were crossed.

The inside of your ear
is a stained red sun catcher and

every way I twisted fit
to make your pillow.

We are thin and
our ribs strike through
our skin
the same way
when we speak

in your arms,
the green veins curl
down the soft strong muscle,
to where I wake up cradled
in your palm.

The smooth plateau of my belly
rises and scoops inside when I breathe.

Facing you,
my navel is open.

Your eyes open,
always the ocean,
where the puddles
reflect my brown eyes.

Our limbs are
twisted,

young roots
sprawled across
a warm earth.

**Vertical Connection**

Eternity is the scent of your sweat
erasing in the sweet static of sleep.
From the full and hollow inside
of the mind I watch electric veins
stretch to make red skies,
connecting my lips to your eyes.

Desire is the thick liquid midnight
swimming sweet like acid
in trickling gold circuits.
In between scenes I reach with the need
to hold rubber flesh to remind me of the same
slick tingle you whisper
in mounting decibels till I shine.

At dawn, honey colored acid clouds
wash my eyelids clean.
All that remain are the long detonated
red and yellow wires
of recorded promises.

**Guitar Strings**

A good player
plucks each strand stretched across her
gaping mouth until it vibrates,
and caresses her
chords more

and whispers to her inside,
that dark whole,
then taps her belly more
when she's in the mood.

He is learning
the way to match her voice
to her rising pulse
until it sings,
until it forgives.

He knows.
He listens
for the voice that resounds

from inside where no one
has ever seen the inside
of a guitar

or my body, curved in the smiling yes
of my hips,
because he has learned.

**Moon Crown**

To greet the moon at its crowning,
carved of cold and soul and bone is to remember words
you spoke when you loved me, when you were me, I held you
as much as I could gather cradled in my lap and let you cry out
the doubt from deep inside the first woman you ever loved
who left you when she left your father and you
were old enough to remember
but not old enough
not to need her

and it was the right decision to leave
the triangle you and the other woman made
I tell myself
you played that way
because your mother left you
nothing which teaches nothing
except how not to be
and you swore
she wouldn't be a problem anymore
except you didn't tell her
who I was so all she did was come
again and again as if she loved you. My solace
is the good chance she'll disintegrate too
like diesel clouds before
the cold bone moon.

**For Eros, Love Psyche**

In my process of becoming,
when all your absence aches,
you will become a stranger
and end the stop
you've made.

And when all the affection
we have given
has folded shut forever,

let it be said
when I have become
this stranger, you have been
a flame around my heart,
a lantern I lost
along the way to becoming what
Fate has chosen us
to be.

## The Bitter End

I passed through The Bitter End,
a pub underground on New Year's Eve.

I hear they're burning effigies in Ecuador.

In the street there is immense logic after all,
when they paste old lovers' jeans on a doll,
and throw cologne scented towels
around it so it burns like the Old Year.

From the balcony of my grandmother's house,
I watched behind silk curtains,
and frowned like an atheist
as the body fell to ashes
to burn the year away.

Back home in Manhattan,
I would like to patch the months
around a mannequin,
in puppet strings and rent checks
and hair of salted seaweed
from the wasted bays of Boston,

to burn
across the strings of a bass guitar,
striking and striking
midnight.

## Walking Around Cambridge

On my right, I walk to the window
of the Ethiopian restaurant
where we once loved
to feed each other
inside, our fingers warm with injera,
tender sheets to gather sweet
spiced meat, each time leaving behind
the frost and slate cold sky,
remote as the chance of a fathom
measuring the space between clouds.

It is hours before
chairs open around each messob,
woven with red and orange whirlwinds.

I didn't notice, at first, the triangle
torn from a watercolor blue map
stuck to the meeting
of two walls in a tight corner,

or the mouth of the ebony mask
carved in pointed no
below the ceiling painted rust red
above the empty glasses.

But this time I turn my back, as if
there never was a night of red wine
that stained anyone's tongue—
yours or hers
or mine.

**Sonnet in Contemplation of Hieronymus Bosch's**
*Death and the Miser*

The miser's chamber once held sacred wealth,
a lover's fingers, he kissed as in prayer
to the Queen, she believed, in his puce lair.
The wily priest's decade mocks him in stealth.

Of a passion turned faith, her letters telth.
Baalim vermin fall to read of her fair
bequeath of grapes, his return of seed bare
to her sinuous lips, toasting his health.

Armet and lance never made him a knight
so he nailed gold grape bundles to his arc,
one for each decade of her resigned flight,
content now to offer Death coins, the mark
on his soul for Her quill, to end his plight,
as Love's light shaft and he pass into dark.

**In the Room**

The trains I interrupt when waking
in the new room are thoughts I should leave
to the cackling of tracks overnight.

As I cleaned the wretched window
I thought I saw a bird, collapsed
on the fire escape,
its green head curled to meet
a weathered chest
tangled in cables the gentle rain rusted
and battered.

It was a rag nestled over
its twisted skin.
I dreamt I chewed its veins as I slept.

I burned a candle on each windowsill,
the matron raspberry
round glass giving
black vapor to the corners
rising first with no
scent save the embers.
It would take days
to bring the sweet.

The quiet yellow candle
from my lover's fingers
sits with long faded smoke rings
that used to caress the air—
his countenance and cries lay trapped
in gentle glass.
He promised nothing
more than black smoke scented with vanilla
as an afterthought.

Embers sit on the windowsill,
filled with enough love to burn
another time.

**The Same Cold**

I smell the cold winds
from the back porch in this new room.
It's the same wooden staircase
where I smoked the same cigarettes
drowned in rain on the back porch.

There was a little clay bowl,
I remember
the night the vapors blew white
in the cold wind,
the kind that imbues
the soul where the bones blow
cold as the same planes
that roar between eternal stars
where you kissed me once,
beneath them.

It is the same
cold wet wind
but I am nowhere
near the ocean
in October.

Tonight I swirled the ashes
of a new
cigarette like tea
in a chipped cup,
its imperfect red
spots look nothing
like stars or
spinning red leaves
in October.

I have returned
to the cold clinging wind
nowhere near an ocean.
But it's the same back porch
in this room
I thought was not
full of smoke
and you.

**Tapas**

Endless plates of Jamón Serrano straddle
yellow wedges of tortilla poked
with toothpicks at the bar.

And the winged petals of the dancer's dress
shake the boot prints out of the air vents,
with a polka dot flourish
fanning at the door
because lovers are as many as tapas,
endless plates of flesh,
salted with sweat, soaked in cologne
endless plates thickened with milk
that stains the carpet and pillows.

And just as there is more
of the menu,
all kinds of meat
and sweet pungent cheese
sit on the tongue.
There is more love to speak of
until the next choosing.

**Homecoming**

The pulsing trains of my City
stream the same currents
through the Western sand dunes
in their eternal struggle to kiss
the elusive red sunset.

And each time the Pacific thrusts you back
to me the fireworks blossom
alongside the Queensboro Bridge.
You once said it smelled like home here.

You may find that you love
water towers too,
those lonely fedoras hidden
on the dust-lined shelves
of Times Square.

Blue moons will continue to circulate
across the pulsing skyline,
adorned with oversized fire bulbs, lighted flowers.
Those are the mechanisms,
the reasons,
behind the pulse
inside my thumb, my whole heart
and you, my whole heart.

Before you arrive at the Golden Gate,
urging away from Times Square,
know the entire pulse of my City,
my whole heart,
awaits you.

**Fire Leaves**

At sunset the trees come
calling from their concrete beds,
waving red peacock feathers
at the cargo trains that carry only the promise
of running down the lace metal gates of the bridge,
all the way West,
as if to say come closer
to where the Sun straddles
the East River's mouth
before dropping a bulb
into the streetlamp's eye.
When I recline
on a feathered red comforter,
the thought of you coming
back to watch the fire kiss the East
River makes it possible
to connect every parallel
current beneath us.

**Simple Morning**

Love stood over the bed in the morning
in his soft white undershirt,
before shaving his angelic skin
with that easy grin
that says of course
what came before
was only a nightmare
and in the same breath
kissed me awake
and awake.

You brought me chamomile tea
the morning after the party.
And after we danced,
you let me dance alone a bit
the way you know I like.
You make me laugh
when you tell me the things I say
the way I say them
in my whiny voice
and never hold a drop of it against me.

I've never known anyone
who wanted all my happiness.
That just is
what you do best.

You are the sunlight in my soul
and the silence
to every doubt.

There is the wind,
there is the sky and

loving you
is simple.

**In the quiet**

I find you in the quiet
wash of sun blankets
covering the boulevard
each morning
after morning

meditating on the blue
cold between clouds
I find the silent answers
to the loud anxious tangles
that are only shouts of dust
blowing away

when broken too often
the war stops in and outside
your embrace alone
silences my burn and you

are the new day
that stays.

**Rain Arrangement**

I wake up before becoming
the worker mother wife
far from the husband who took
that last minute business trip to Europe
as though it were involuntary

every time he says
everybody wants to go home.

The shadows spilling through the blinds
this morning mean rain

on the walk to the elevated train
after static strides
toward our son's school, I'll explain
they'll be seeing more of me in the mornings.

On my side of the bed,
I lie like my father did
in the bed he shared with my mother,
with the same long pale legs, waiting
all day until she returned, I imagine
what it must have been like for him
all those hours, anchored to his side of the bed,
shrouded in rain shadows
spilling through the same
shut blinds.

My son snores in whistles
through the chill of wet leaves
wafting through his window
and I doubt

my husband's red brick pillow filling in the gap
between his bed and the window
will stop him from rolling out
like last time.

I slide my legs out of bed
then curse the betrayal
of the creak in the floor,
because my son will awaken and want
more milk play time and me, and
I go because it's what my mother would have
done with certainty if I don't
he'll die.

He sleeps unstirred,
with long pale legs stretched across the red comforter,
the one my husband bought me
because it was my favorite color and big enough
to pull over his blue and white striped blanket on his side
to make it look unified, just
as I said I wanted.

In the hallway, I cross back into the gray
spotlight beneath the slanted roof pane
staving off the crash of the insistent rain.

## Doors

In the viscous dark
that adorns every room in this house
we'll leave
sooner than we thought
we would
I called out goodbye
since you'd be gone
in the morning

I found a reason to go out and buy
milk, melon, chocolate anything,
one of the few things of value
my father taught me to do instinctively
the way everyone else has
a tic to buy a house
as obvious as having
skim milk in the fridge
and a car in the garage
when he never learned to drive
the neighbors said

he was never a man
before my mother
in the sense
of use
to the point of being the one
to bring home the kind of bread
she deserved.

So she was the one
who scraped together
all she saved from what would have been
a computer, a house, a kept car
to buy a corporate share flat
no one could tell her
to leave for any lie
or any reason.

And when I return to the silent
still certain dark
with my offering of milk
and a honeydew melon
dripping with sweet
from the smell of it

I see you've avoided the dread
of my key click

and when you can't hold it anymore
from the single lamp-lit den I listen
to the sound of opening,
then closing

door to closing door.

**Anniversary**

In Germany, they congratulate you on your birthday
and your anniversary, as if
to say it's an accomplishment
to remain another year, unbroken.

I chose a restaurant near Strawberry Fields
because it's the only place that's ours
from all those years ago when the guitarists improvised,
as we improvised lunch and dinner every night before
he was supposed to leave.

But he stayed and we declared
Strawberry Fields was ours.

I sat across from him in the booth
but indented an inch on my side.
We came despite the involuntary
sparring last night, as every night.

I stuffed my mouth with fennel shards
mixed with lemon and orange fragments
beneath a raft of skin crisp bass, charred enough;
I looked up between bites to smile, as if
to say thanks for showing.

Afterwards he didn't want to walk to the Park
to find the new guitarists
because never again could we tread as we
did, matched shadows,
ambling past and over
Imagine.

**Static**

If I pull back, further,
to the place where static starts,
the beginning is the blue even
before the past,
where I might have to strain to listen
between the purple and orange dust
particles for where I think lovers go
when they go.

So the buzzing sunlight
on the porch the first time
you called me bright
sunlight is the only place
I find you
in those afternoons where as dizzy
as the sticking sun hung,
the gray rain stayed
in the darkest ether
embers poised in the Heavens to fall,
and it did
fall.

If I strain all the way back to the place
where pain is the only place, anyway,
I can find you,
I strain
because (you wouldn't
believe me if I told you)
I read the static better now.

I might say
I wish I knew you now
I wish
and all my strings shake
with wishing.

**Star Drop**

Outside in the still frost
quiet night I heard
an incessant tapping

like a runner's steps
or a giant clock
or a hundred ice drops

plopping in a vat
one
by one
by one
to hit the tin pan
someone left between the broken
ice tiles when they left.

The mistake implies haste

like an old lover driving off
in the coal gray night
plotted once with the silence
of ecstatic and endless stars.

## The Day before Valentine's Day

I once loved a man
born on Valentine's Day.
He was the only one.
And every time I see aluminum
red balloon hearts, full of breath, floating up,
just to tangle in the gray
branches, long stripped
of every dead leaf,
ecstatic at the rushes and the bite
the wind offers, my throat tightens, less
at the memory of the one
who once held my whole heart,
but at the possibility of never again
believing a heart can float
down an ice-glazed street.

**Psyche's Sunday**

The day arrived
with bright blind of sun,
and hanging ache
in the sky after weeks of gray
rain and love songs,
next after next,
like the days that have arrived,
one after the other,
since I left you.

But the day arrives in Sunday quiet
shadows when the house goes dark
and all that's left is me,
the one that's become without you,
the one
sitting in the dark I chose
before love songs,
each relevant and bright,

right on about broken love and the stagnant no
that sits in my memory, my punishment
for the balance of my days,
the answer in the still dark no
to my bright,
whole desire,
my eternal castigation
for the day I denied the entire
bright sun.

**Vibrations**

We used to bang like piano keys,
headboard clapping, white walls shaking,
moaning notes in deep crescendo, upside down,
so far down, the downstairs neighbor wrote
a single note to say please stop the noise
and those midnight vibrations.

After another fight
with the man I said was better
for me I lie in the empty
Queen-sized bed in the red
comforter sham he bought me for my birthday
years ago when it was easier to buy me
things and I listen to the moan of young love
on the other side of white walls quaking
in deep crescendo.

Afterwards she sings and he laughs
and she laughs and now
the moon is the only one
who knows I think of you and how
we used to bang
like piano keys.

**Reservoirs**

So they pass away, lovers,
in the reservoir of memories washed and
washed back again
alongside black train tunnels
rewinding all the time.

And it's sad
but sadder still
that they rush away
with the significance
of those waves;
those white-spittled caps
that keep coming
and replacing
the rushing applause
of water.
The gathered ores of love become
residue in the rushing.

I think of you in the same flashes
of water that rise in the proud
grooves around my eyes
after all the months
of water rising up
too many times.

I run alongside
the reservoirs now,
when the sun pinks over
in hazy orange veils,
and glides around the river,
dizzy and beautiful,
or nauseating, as you prefer.

I wish you could see
the woman running around it,
safely a stranger.

I wish I could forget all the waves that made you,
all the days that made us
drowned over,
in memory,
in reservoirs.

## Appendix Heart

Afterwards, all that remains
is a prickly pear scar, twelve blood-red seeds
plotted along a thermometer
of yoked sun streaks and a purple road
stitched high above my thigh
like a grin that refuses to break.

In the countless convalescent hours,
I meditate on the same scar
that lives inside long ago
songs about lost
lovers in the desert space
where they congregate
to pick cactus fruit and wait
until it's time to return.

Most never return.
But once in a parallel while,
a voice calls from the hollow
left where there used to be
an organ born to ruin,
sutured only with the promise of undying
love, turned prickly sweet.

## Cherimoya Heart

When it's time to eat my heart-
shaped cherimoya, custard apple,
like Eve, like Musetta, who, in the libretto
according to Marcello, *mangia il cuore*,

I slide my thumbs into my widow's peak, pausing
before cracking back walls of green scales,
tin-shiny, hard-nippled,

run my fingers along the wet
valves of tender novaculite,
dripping with perfume of pear and passionfruit,

then dip between my folded lips
to remove every venomous
seed, useless and lethal,
so that all that remains is my tongue suckling sweet
fangs from my fingertips,

sticky and at times acrid,
having scraped at times too close to the skin,
but each time, I never needed anyone
to know my predilection
for metamorphic creation.

Stephanie Laterza is a writer and attorney from Brooklyn, New York. Born in Astoria, Queens and recently relocated to Park Slope, Stephanie has been a storyteller and creative writer for as long as she can remember. She holds a B.A. in English from Fordham College at Lincoln Center and a J.D. from New England Law School, where a course in Law and Literature brought her full circle to her love of writing. Her love of poetry can be traced back to her childhood, when she received a copy of Shel Silverstein's *Where the Sidewalk Ends*, which introduced her to the basics of poetic lyricism as well as the power of words to convey both personal and universal themes. Stephanie has admired and been inspired most by the poetry of Dr. Maya Angelou, Langston Hughes, Pablo Neruda, Lucille Clifton, W.H. Auden, and U.S. Poet Laureate Tracy K. Smith. Stephanie's favorite fiction writers include Jhumpa Lahiri, Isabel Allende, Paulo Coelho, Gabriel García Márquez, and others.

Stephanie's background as an attorney inspired her feminist legal thriller, *The Boulevard Trial*, which, in a review featured in North of Oxford Press and Compulsive Reader, poet Karen Corinne Herceg has described as, "a good, fast-paced read with more than a few lessons to impart." Stephanie is the recipient of a SU-CASA 2018 artist-in-residence award from the Brooklyn Arts Council, and her poetry has been published in *L'Éphémère Review, First Literary Review-East, A Gathering of the Tribes, Ovunque Siamo, Newtown Literary, Literary Mama, San Francisco Peace and Hope,* and *Meniscus Magazine*. Her short fiction has been featured in *The Nottingham Review, Obra/Artifact, Akashic Books, Writing Raw,* and *Literary Mama*.

When not writing, Stephanie can be found raising her precocious and indefatigable son, Alex, and thanking her supernaturally supportive husband, Florian.

www.ingramcontent.com/pod-product-compliance
Lightning Source LLC
LaVergne TN
LVHW041504070426
835507LV00012B/1310